A Guided Meditation
for Beginners

The ancient techniques described in this book have been used for thousands of years by many teachers and gurus from all over the world. Read each page in its entirety and follow the instructions exactly as they are written. Do not proceed to the next page until the instruction has been fully completed. DO NOT SKIP ANY PAGES. The meditation provided is self paced, however it is recommended to set aside at least 10 minutes of uninterrupted time in order to have a complete experience. The instructions are formatted in a way which is intended to be clear and easy to follow for meditators of all skill levels. Some beginners may encounter the urge to skip ahead, but it is very important not to skip any pages and not to move forward until the instruction on each page has been fully completed.

Inhale.

Exhale.

Inhale.

Exhale.

Inhale.

Exhale.

Inhale.

Exhale.

Inhale.

Exhale.

Inhale.

Exhale.

Inhale.

Exhale.

Inhale.

Exhale.

Inhale!

Exhale!

Inhale.

Exhale.

Inhale.

Exhale.

Inhale.

Exhale.

Inhale.

Exhale.

Inhale.

Exhale.

Inhale.

Exhale.

Inhale.

Exhale.

Inhale.

Exhale.

Inhale.

Exhale.

Inhale.

Exhale.

Inhale.

Exhale.

Repeat as necessary.

Made in the USA
Coppell, TX
23 June 2021

57974936R00026